Dyslexia and the iPad

Overcoming Dyslexia With Technology

James and Linda Nuttall

Published by James Nuttall and Linda Nuttall

License Notes

Introduction

Sharing Lessons From Life

Hello, we are Jim and Linda Nuttall. We wish to welcome you to our book. This book is about Jim, his dyslexia and the iPad. Linda has provided very helpful writing assistance. When speaking using I, we are referring to Jim.

I am dyslexic. While growing up, I knew that I had a reading problem. During elementary school and high school, I struggled to read. I was basically a nonreader. Every day, I watched my family and fellow students read books, magazines and newspapers. I longed to do the same. When I went away to college, I visited the University of Chicago Reading Clinic. At this clinic I learned that I had dyslexia. I persevered with college and earned a Ph.D. in Psychology from Michigan State University.

This short book is about dyslexia and the Apple iPad and some additional technologies. Over the years, I learned some tricks for coping with dyslexia, many of which are enhanced by recently developed technologies. I would like to pass these tricks on to you. If you or your child has dyslexia, I hope you find this book helpful. You do not need to read this book from front to back. You can skip around, reading what you like.

Why the iPad

Steve Jobs called the iPad a "revolutionary and magical" device. Little did he or Apple realize that the iPad would revolutionize education. Little did they realize that the iPad would be a magical device for both children and adults with dyslexia. As I grew up, I could not read books. I could not read newspapers or encyclopedias. I longingly looked at stacks of magazines outside my ability to read. The world of knowledge was closed to me. The Apple iPad has changed all of that. The iPad, a miracle in my hands, lets me read books, newspapers, webpages, magazines and blogs. Fortunately, Apple and Steve Jobs build the iPad to be accessible to individual with handicapping characteristics. In this book we outline how the iPad revolutionizes the lives of dyslexic children and adults. Along the way, we discuss a variety of techniques for improving reading and writing skills for people with dyslexia. Many of these techniques can be applied even without the latest technology. But I find the iPad especially enhances the coping skills presented in the book.

We hope you enjoy this book and benefit from the iPad as much as Jim has. Feel free to email us (iPadandDyslexia@gmail.com) and share your iPad stories and point out your favorite apps.

Chapter 1: Dyslexia—the Experience

What is Dyslexia?

Wikipedia defines dyslexia as follows: "Dyslexia is a very broad term defining a learning disability that impairs a person's fluency in reading, and is marked with a difficulty in phonological awareness, phonological decoding, orthographic coding, auditory short-term memory, or rapid naming."

Here is the list of attributes that often represent dyslexia.

Difficulty Matching Sounds to Letters

A dyslexic child often has difficulty learning the alphabet and matching the letters with their sounds. Often in elementary school dyslexic students sit and struggle over letters and word sounds. Even as an adult a dyslexic individual may still struggle with unfamiliar or highly technical words.

Difficulty Hearing Sounds in Words

Dyslexic individuals often have difficulty sounding out words. When presented with unfamiliar words, dyslexic individuals have extreme difficulty sounding out the word. Even as adults, it is hard for dyslexic individuals to sound out scientific names of medications. I frequently say that the television game show Wheel of Fortune is a dyslexic's nightmare.

Difficulty Analyzing Words into Syllables and Whole Units

Fluent readers frequently analyze syllables and words quickly at a subconscious level simply by sight. This automatic process often does not happen for people with dyslexia. When asked to divide words into syllables, a dyslexic person painstakingly guesses to identify syllables.

Reading Is Labored and Slow

One of the hallmarks of dyslexia is very labored and slow reading. When in school, dyslexic students often read only a fraction of an assignment which others breeze through.

Difficulty Remembering New Words

During reading lessons dyslexic students often do not recognize words which they have just read. These students often hear the teacher say, "Remember, we just had that word."

Easily Looses Place While Reading

In class, when read round-robin, dyslexic students often loose their place and cannot find where others are reading. Even as adults dyslexic individuals complain about losing their place on the page while reading.

Subvocalizes when Reading

Dyslexic students frequently say the words quietly to themselves as they are reading. This is called subvocalization. Fast fluent readers do not subvocalize.

4

Fluent readers recognize words by sight. Word meaning is instantaneous, with no sounding out of the words. A dyslexic individual often must say the word in his mind in order to obtain meaning.

Short-Term Memory Deficit

Dyslexic individuals often have a short-term serial memory deficit. While struggling to learn to read, a dyslexic student often forgets what is being read. For example, the student does not remember the beginning of the sentence by the time she gets to the end of the sentence.

Difficulty Remembering Names and Phone Numbers

Dyslexic individuals are embarrassed not to remember people's names. When people are introduced, a dyslexic individual clearly hears the name. However, when asked to remember the name, the name cannot be recalled. This is also true of phone numbers.

Difficulty Learning the Multiplication Table

Dyslexic students are often the last ones in their class to learn the multiplication table.

Extreme Difficulty with Foreign Languages

Foreign languages classes are extremely difficult for dyslexic students. Phrase books and computerized software are often no help. When listening to a foreign language, the language just sounds like an endless stream of gobbledygook. As a native English speaker, I say, "The most difficult foreign-language that I ever learned was —**English**."

Dyslexia and Reading Research

Dr. Sally Shaywitz, M.D., is the director of the Yale Center for Dys¥lexia and Creativity. She is a professor at the Yale University Medical School. The Yale center specializes in research on dyslexia and reading. She studies how the brain process reading. Dr. Shaywtiz places individuals in a MRI machine and asks them to read text projected on a screen. Using functional magnetic resonance imaging (fMRI) scans of the brain, she maps out the brain activity while the person reads. Her work shows that there are three primary areas of the brain used for reading.

Parts of the Human Brain

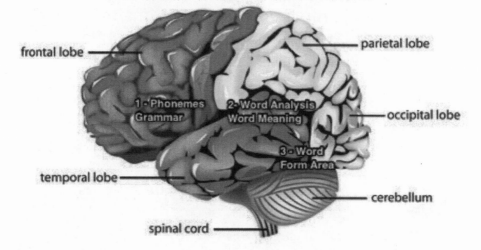

frontal lobe

parietal lobe

1 - Phonemes Grammar

2 - Word Analysis Word Meaning

occipital lobe

3 - Word Form Area

temporal lobe

cerebellum

spinal cord

The first area for reading is in the front part of the brain. This area of the brain is known as Broca's area. Broca's area is important in recognizing speech

sounds. Speech sounds come in units called phonemes. Words are made up of these speech units.
The letters of our alphabet stand for these phonemes. The frontal area #1 pictured in the diagram is
used for phoneme analysis. In early reading, students
are taught about phoneme sounds. This is called
phonological awareness. In reading, decoding letters
is associated with matching speech sounds to the letters. Understanding the letters and sounds is the first
step in reading; this happens in Broca's area.

The second area #2 pictured in the diagram is in the
temporal lobe. The temporal lobe is important in the
perception of speech. This area is known as
Wernike's area. Wernike's area is also related to recognizing written words. This area helps in recognition
of word parts and segments like syllables, prefixes
and suffices. This is important in understanding language syntax or meaning. So, this area is important
in analyzing a word and its parts.

The third area for reading, #3, is located in an area
overlapping both the visual and the auditory cortex.
This area of the brain is related to rapid and automatic word recognition. This is the area of the brain
most useful for fast fluent reading.

Beginning readers rely heavily on the front area of the
brain to match sounds and letters. As one becomes
better in reading, the two back areas of the brain are
used more. The second area helps in analyzing
words to make sense out of them. The third area is a
rapid unconscious process for quick recognition of

words. Rapid reading especially relies on this third area of the brain.

The fMRI studies of non-dyslexic readers show that they use all three areas while reading. As a person gets better at reading, the two back areas are used most. The fMRI images of dyslexic readers show a different pattern. Dyslexic readers show a high level of activity in the front #1 area of the brain. The two back areas are not used as much. So both adults and children with dyslexia have a greater reliance on the frontal phonemic analysis area. Dyslexic readers primarily use sounding out words as their way of reading. By not using the word analysis and rapid recognition areas, dyslexic readers are often slow readers. Some research shows that early systematic reading instruction for dyslexic children can increase the use of the word analytic and rapid recognition areas during reading. Dr. Shaywitz's book, *Overcoming Dyslexia*, is available in the Kindle Store, the iBookstore or from Bookshare.

Chapter 2: Reading and School

Learning to Read

People all over the world learn to speak a language. From birth, children are surrounded by people speaking their native language. Fortunately, as children, we come with a biological propensity to learn this language. Within the first year of life, we start to make the sounds or building blocks of our language. In the second year, we start using words. By the time we reach kindergarten, we are language experts. We can talk about our world and make our desires known simply by speaking.

Speaking is a marvelous process. For most of us, speaking requires very little effort and is natural.

Reading is a language-based skill. Humanity took many millennia before inventing reading and writing. Writing is a means for putting down symbols which stand for language. As a writer thinks of ideas, she puts down the symbols representing her speech. When these symbols are decoded, one can reconstruct her speech and understand her ideas.

Although reading is closely related to speaking, reading is not as natural as speaking. Our biology is programmed to learn to speak and understand what is spoken to us. Reading, on the other hand, must be carefully taught. Children have to spend many hours and years being taught to read. Reading is primarily a process of decoding written symbols which stand for spoken language. Once decoded, the child must construct these symbols into meaningful ideas.

People in different cultures use different symbols to stand for written language. In English we use the 26 letters of the English alphabet to construct written language. These letters and letter combinations stand for the 46 sounds, phonemes, of our language. When one looks at letters, this fact is not obvious.

For years there has been a debate about how to teach reading. Some professionals stressed learning letters and the phonemes of language, i.e., phonics. Others emphasized whole language, in which words are comprehended as units within the meaningful structure of language. The fMRI research of the brain by Dr. Sally Shaywitz, M.D., helps clarify this debate. Three areas of the brain are used during reading. First an area for analyzing the speech-phoneme units of print is used. Second an area for analyzing the parts and wholes of print are used. Lastly, a third area quickly evaluates the words as a whole and comprehends word meanings. So we can see from Shaywitz' research, reading is understanding print as phonemes, parts and wholes. These three aspects of reading are used by readers. No part should be excluded or ignored.

The following topics are generally presented in school when teaching children to read.

Print Awareness. The first step in learning to read is to understand that print stands for speech. For example, when a parent reads a book, the child understands the print on the page is the story. The story goes from the front of the book to the back of the book. There is a top and a bottom to the book. After a while the child knows the words go from left to right. Often the first "words" recognized are store signs. The Golden Arches M stands for McDonalds.

iPad Book Apps That Are Read Aloud Experiences. There are literally hundreds of great read along children's books in the App Store. Just search for "children's books."

• Jack and the Bean Stock
• Goldie Locks and the Three Bears
• Miss Spiders Tea Party
• The Monster at the End of This Book

Alphabet Principle. Often the next step is learning to recognize and name the letters of the alphabet. My grandson learned some of his letters by typing on the iPad keyboard. After opening the YouTube app, he wanted to know which letters to type to find Tom and Jerry cartoons. Children learn to recognize and name both upper case and lower case letters. Lastly, they learn that the letters stand for speech sounds. There are a large number of iPad apps that teach the ABCs. Here are a few of my favorites.

ABC GoGo FlashCards—ABC GoGo FlashCards app shows each letter of the alphabet in bright colors on a flash card. When the card is tapped, it says the letter. Tap the card a second time and it flips to show a picture matching the letter. For instance, "A" is matched with "airplane."

ABC 123—ABC 123 app teaches letters and numbers with naming and writing practice. There is writing practice for both capital and small letters. Letter names are read aloud. Using a stylus gives writing practice, like using a pencil. Each letter or number has guidance for writing. This is a favorite fun app of my grandson.

First Letters and Phonics—First Letters and Phonics is a talking alphabet book. You match the letters and the app says their name with associated picture.

Phonemic Awareness. Phonemic awareness is becoming aware that the words we speak are made up of speech sounds. For example, the word cat is made up of three sounds: /c/, /a/, and /t/. Phonemic awareness is more a listening activity than seeing activity. You can play saying the sounds of words. Like you can say Nana, /N/, /a/, /n/, /a/. You can also clap for every sound you hear. Then it is helpful to try to identify the first sound in a word.

Dr Seuss ABC—Dr Seuss ABC is an exceptional introductory ABC book. Besides saying the alphabet letter, it then repeats words that begin with the letter.

ABC Phonics Animals—ABC Phonics Animals gives letter naming and writing practice on both upper and lower case letters. A word mode can be chosen which uses the letter as the initial sound of a word.

"W" is matched with "Walrus." There is also a companion app *ABC Write Zoo Animals*.

Phonics. Phonics systematically teaches the relationships between letters and letter combinations and their associated sounds. The English language uses 46 sounds. They are the sounds related to each letter of the alphabet. The English vowels have a hard and a soft sound. Then there are combinations or blends of sounds such as /ch/, /th/, or /wh/.

Preschool University—Preschool University has a variety of apps to help teach early reading. They have eight different free apps in their "ACB Magic" series. These apps are appropriate for kindergarten through second grade. *ABC Magic* helps to teach the phonetic sound associated with each letter of the alphabet. Each letter sound is paired with a picture. Then there are *ABC Reading* and *ABC Spelling,* which help teach long and short vowel sounds and consonant blends.

Pocket Phonics—Pocket Phonics presents each letter of the alphabet by saying its sound. Additionally, as the letter is introduced, a line traces how to write the letter. So your child can match sound and practice writing.

Phonics Genius—Phonics Genius is a very complete phonics teacher. Many phonics combinations are presented. This app would work best with older students grade 3 and above.

Sounding Out Words. After letters are learned, sounding out words comes next. You can take short three letter words to start sounding out practice. You can count the letters. As you and your child look at a word, make a sound for each letter. Then repeat saying the word.

Build A Word—Build A Word shows and sounds out words. The player matches letters and sounds to build the word.

PBPhonics—PBPhonics is a great app that shows and practices sounding out words.

iSpy Phonics—iSpy Phonics lets you build your own phonics picture cards. You choose a picture of Mommy and record /M/ommy.

Word Wizard—Word Wizard allows you to type or arrange words. Then the words are spoken. You can also create your own word lists.

Sound Beginnings is a bridge between phonetic sounds and hearing them in words. There is practice for beginning, middle, and ending sounds.

Little Reader 3 Letters—Little Reader 3 Letters you match words with pictures. When the word is tapped, it is pronounced. Even though these are three-letter words, the vocabulary can be challenging.

Sight Words. There are a number of words that are easiest to learn by sight. Words such as "the," "and", "can," "for",,and "in." These words have been compiled in lists for each grade. You can find them by looking for Dolch list. The Dolch list is a collection of common words that do not easily match pictures and are difficult to teach by phonics.

Build A Word—Build A Word is a multi-modal word-spelling app. You see and hear the word and move letters around to spell the word. You can build your own lists. This is a well-designed app

Ladybug Sight Words—The Ladybug Sight Words presents a group of sight words on the backs of lady-bugs on a leaf. When your child selects the correct word, the ladybug scurries off the leaf.

Ace Writer—Ace Writer Dolch Sight Word is a multi-modal presentation. Your child sees the word, hears the word spoken, and practices writing the word. Multi-modal approaches are often effective. When-ever I want to learn a word, I have to see, hear and write it a number of times.

Spelling Free—Spell Free allows you to build a list of your own words. The app pronounces the word. I just wish the font were larger.

Vocabulary. As your child reads more and more, she finds new unfamiliar words. At first, most of the words your child reads refer to familiar things. But after kin-dergarten and first grade, books contain new unfamil-iar words. The meaning of these words must be ex-plained and learned. So, you should talk about these words and their meaning. You should also practice reading these words several times. By the time a child is in forth grade, much of the reading in school contains many new words. The iPad offers a number of illustrated book apps that can read the story aloud as your child reads along. These enhanced ebooks help to introduce vocabulary in a fun and stimulating manner.

Enhanced ebook apps in the App Store

• 'Twas the Night Before Christmas
• The Hare and The Turtle
• Cat in the Hat
• The Tale of Peter Rabbit
• Miss Spiders Tea Party

Fluency. Fluency is generally defined as smooth silent reading. Some also include reading with appropriate meaning and emotional expression. Fluency comes with a lot of practice. There is the practice of sounding out words and recognizing sight words. More practice means faster recognition of words. As fluency increases, it is easier to comprehend what is read. One of the major ways to build fluency is to do a good deal of reading. Children and teenagers often like to read book series. Book series are very helpful in building fluency since vocabulary and themes frequently repeat themselves. Textbooks, on the other hand, are very poor at building fluency. Book series are available for the iPad from the iBookstore. If your child has difficulty reading, have these series read aloud using the iPad built-in VoiceOver reader.

• Curious George New Adventures
• Percy Jackson & the Olympians Series by Rick Ri-

ordan

- Junie B. Jones Series
- The Mysterious Benedict Society
- Judy Moody by Megan McDonald (Bookshare)
- Hank the Cowdog Series

For more suggestions on book series look up www.kidsbookseries.com.

Silent reading. After some time, readers can recognize words by sight. The very proficient readers I have talked to say that they read totally silently. They do not hear the words in their minds as they read. These readers often read 300 or more words per minute. Many people never reach this proficiency. Others remark that reading is saying the words in their mind. For this latter group, they often deny that true silent reading exists. True silent reading does exist.

Whenever, I meet a very proficient silent reader, I like to interview him or her. Most individuals I have interviewed say that their reading greatly improved as they spent time reading. Throughout elementary and middle school, they often read easy but highly enjoyable books. Often these books were a serialized set of short novelettes. Vocabulary and characters often repeated themselves. Some say they read a lot of comic books. I stress the reading was easy and quickly comprehended. *And they did a lot of it.*

In high school such readers often spent time reading mysteries or science fiction. Over time, the reading became more complex. Reading included literature.

One thing their reading did NOT include was a preponderance of textbook reading. Most dyslexic and poor readers generally read only the textbooks assigned for homework. In my experience, focusing on textbook reading does not lead to fluency. Reading for pleasure leads to fluency and silent reading. Again, the best results are achieved by reading series books (see Fluency).

Comprehension. The ultimate goal of reading is to comprehend what the author has written. My guide for increasing comprehension is to read something more than once. The second reading will be more fluent. More fluency relates to better comprehension. When you read something a second time, you will be amazed at what you missed on the first reading.

Frequently, teacher guides emphasize teaching students to ask questions as they read. These guides also emphasize making prediction about what might come next. I do agree it is helpful to read the questions or headings at the beginning of a chapter. But as to the rest, I am mystified. In my interviews with proficient readers, they say that they neither ask questions nor make predictions.

Another means to increase comprehension is to read the entire story, article or chapter. Frequently, in school students are taught to skim for answers. The best trick to comprehension is reading. My daughter often wanted to read only the few pages assigned by the teacher. I would persevere and we would read the entire chapter. Reading the entire chapter more often than not was the right decision.

To increase comprehension, first read books that are at or slightly above your child's reading ability. By frequently reading these books, comprehension will increase. If your child has high comprehension but low reading level, search out High/Low books to read. These books have a high interest but place less demand on the reading.

- High/Low Books
- Hurricane Song
- Storm Runners

Response to Intervention

When students are having difficulty learning to read, schools are required to help. Different approaches are used to help students learn to read. This is often done in small group instruction with focused teaching and practice in reading. This help is called Response to Intervention (RTI). RTI is not a reading method per se; RTI is a special time set aside for reading instruction. For many struggling readers, this additional small group instruction often works very well. RTI is focuses on children from kindergarten to third grade. A big advantage of the RTI time is that reading instruction and practice are carefully organized and monitored. Students are generally given an extra 30 minutes per day of reading instruction in groups of 3 to 6. Usually RTI lasts for 8 weeks or so. The RTI model stresses doing additional instruction until the student succeeds in reading.

Special Education

When students are not helped by the RTI time, they are often referred for additional help. Dyslexic students may be referred to special education. When this happens, a student is evaluated for a handicapping condition. Dyslexic students are often given the label "Learning Disabled" because of difficulty with reading. Your child may be assigned to spend sometime with a special education teacher. Unfortunately, most special education teachers are not specialists in the teaching of reading. So the special education program often repeats the reading lessons being given in the general classroom. This repetition often does not help. Dyslexic students benefit most from reading programs specifically designed for them, like the Orton-Gillingham method. If your school is lucky enough to have a specialized reading teacher, secure his or her help.

Special Education can be very helpful in a number of ways. When qualified, your child can get extra academic accommodations such as the following:

Special education teachers are good at getting concepts across and often provide extra tutoring.

Recorded audio textbooks can be obtained from Learning Ally.

Digital textbooks are available from your school or from BookShare.org. These digital copies can be read aloud using text-to-speech software.

Sometimes the school will provide a laptop or an iPad to read textbooks aloud. Laptops and iPads can also help with writing and worksheets.

The school may provide speech recognition software to help with writing.

Often students can get extra time on tests.

Tests can be taken in a quiet room with fewer distractions.

Accommodations are made on a case-by-case basis. An Individualized Education Plan (IEP) is developed with input from school personnel and parents. The development of the IEP happens at an IEP meeting. Parents find it helpful to participate in support groups for Learning Disabled students. These groups can often supply advocates who can help you at an IEP meeting. In support groups you can learn about the kinds of accommodations your child needs.

Do not get pushed aside

I remember my third grade teacher placing me in the back row in the furthest desk away from where she sat. In that back seat I could not see the blackboard, nor did I read any of my books. I spent most of the year lost in childhood fantasies not paying attention to the class. At the end of the year, I had made no progress. This teacher told my parents that I was retarded and that I could not learn. Fortunately for me, not until I graduated from college did my parents share what this teacher had said.

Unfortunately, students with hidden disabilities, like dyslexia, are often perceived as being unresponsive learners. Even with legal safeguards, these students are often pushed to one side. If not literally, then figuratively, these students are placed at the back or to the side of the class. If you are the parents of such a child, you will need to work hard to make sure that this does not happen. One of the best things to do is to talk with your child about school every day so that you can review their experiences with them and learn what is happening in school.

Education Laws

Public Law 94-142, the Education for All Handicapped Children Act, was passed in 1975. This law insures that children with disabilities are educated in their local public school instead of being sent to residential institutions or segregated schools. Education has to be accompanied by accommodations to enhance learning.

The Individuals with Disabilities Education Act (IDEA) was passed in 1990. This law insured that children with handicapping conditions should be educated to the *greatest extent possible* with their peers in typical classrooms. IDEA mandated that students with handicapping conditions should have an Individual Education Plan (IEP). Parents or the student's legal guardians were to be always included in IEP development. An IEP includes an identification of the student's handicapping condition. There is also a statement of the student's educational performance. The IEP also sets out the annual goals for educational achievement. It includes a statement of short-term objectives and how instruction will meet the student's educational needs. The IEP specifies if the student needs related services such as speech therapy or technology such as a computer or an iPad. The IEP also states how a student will be integrated in the general classroom.

Even now after over 20 years, teachers still ask, "Why do I have to have students with disabilities in my room." Teachers often have 20 or more students in their classroom. With so many students, teachers are unable to spend individual quality time with any particular student. We wish teachers were not so over worked, but this is a reality. So parents can spend extra quality time with their children at home in the evening.

Rights for Accommodations

Section 504 of the 1973 Rehabilitation Act also provides safeguards and access to school accommodations. Unlike an IEP, which specifies educational goals and instruction, a Section 504 Plan spells out accommodations needed to access education. To be eligible, students must have a disability. It can be physical, mental, emotional or health-related. The disability must interfere with the student's access to an education in the standard school setting. Section 504 guarantees equal access to education for students with disabilities. While an IEP evaluation often shows how a student has an educational gap, under a 504 Plan no gap is required. What is required is an accommodation that allows education to be accessed. Such accommodations may include:

- Help with taking notes
- An extra set of textbooks for home

- Large print
- Assistive technology like laptops
- Extra time on tests

Accommodations After School

The Americans with Disabilities Act (ADA) was also passed in 1990. The ADA gives a legal definition of what "disability" means. The ADA provided for civil rights and safeguards for all individuals with handicapping conditions. Under the ADA, a disability is defined as a "physical or mental impairment that substantially limits one or more major life activities." Major life activities include, but are not limited to, "caring for oneself, performing manual tasks, seeing, hearing, eating, sleeping, walking, standing, lifting, bending, speaking, breathing, learning, reading, concentrating, thinking, communicating, and working."

The ADA was passed to help provide equal opportunity to employment for individuals with a handicapping condition. The ADA requires that employers make "reasonable accommodations" to ensure that an individual with a handicapping condition is able to carry out his/her job functions. This might include modifications to the worksite such as putting in an accessible ramp or handicap bathroom or making changes in a work schedule. The individual may need additional equipment in order to carry out her job. In my case, my employer provided me with software to enlarge what was on my computer screen and also voice dictation software to write reports. Assistive technologies are a "right." They should be used to help individuals with both learning and employment.

Chapter 3: My struggle with dyslexia

My Dyslexia

I have limited vision. As a child I held my books just a few inches from my face while reading. Most teachers and individuals assumed that my great difficulty with reading was due to my poor vision. But I knew people with vision much worst then mine who could read just fine. In the first 12 grades of school, I rarely read anything. In the first five grades, I was oblivious to the fact that I was doing so differently than my fellow students. I spent much of my time daydreaming and thinking about not being in school. I love riding horses, so I often imagined myself riding horses in the Colorado Rocky Mountains.

While in middle school, I first became aware of my difficulties. During sixth grade English, we were working on improving our reading speeds. We had a special book with short readings. The readings were timed in order for us to calculate our reading speed. On the first day, I remember trying to read to the best of my ability. Like the other students, I counted up the number of words that I read and divided by the time spent reading. This gave us our reading speed in words read per minute.

We each announced the number of words per minute read. I read 27 words per minute. The student sitting next to me read 350 words per minute. My teacher then said, "Now in the next reading pull out all of the stops and read as fast as you can." I figured this was my opportunity to shine. So I read as fast as I could. The student sitting next to me now read 600 words per minute. I anxiously calculated my reading speed. I read 33 words per minute. I had gained only five words per minute. All I could do was sit in despair and cry. I finally knew something was dreadfully wrong with my performance in school. To this day I remember this event with great heartache.

To help you understand how catastrophic my reading was, here are the typical reading speeds for elementary students.

Reading Fluency in words per minute:

First grade – 60
Second grade – 70
Third grade – 90
Fourth grade – 120
Fifth grade – 150

Thus in sixth grade I was functioning at half of what a typical first grader could do.

Peer Buddies

In school my classmates and I were given copious amounts of homework with lots of reading. I was totally unable to do this reading. So, at night I would sit in my room sharpening my pencils, arranging my papers and otherwise trying to avoid the reading. I usually got very little done and had nothing to turn in the next day. In order to get by, I would ask my friends what they had read and what they had learned.

These updates kept me going in class. This strategy for learning is now given the name "peer buddies."

Let me tell you a story about peer buddies. My step-daughter, Stephanie, has learning disabilities. We struggled getting the homework done. While she was in middle school, we paid some college students to stay with her during the afternoons. The college students would often sit and do their homework while Stephanie watched television. After some time, Stephanie was sitting there doing homework with the college students. Recently, I read a book for parents of dyslexic students that suggested this peer buddy system for dyslexic kids. Abigail Marshall's *The Everything Parent's Guide To Children With Dyslexia* is available in the Kindle Store and the iBookstore.

Students who struggle with reading and learning can also listen carefully in class. This is a great way to learn. Since I rarely read anything, I especially listened closely in class. On my tests I would write down what I remember my teachers saying. Nowadays if your school will allow it, you can actually record the lectures using a device called the Live Scribe Pen. The Live Scribe Pen is able to sync your hand written notes with the audio portions of the lecture. Also iPad apps like Notability or AudioNote can sync notes with recorded lectures.

University Reading Clinic

When I went away to the university, my father said that I would need readers to read my books to me. "Students with low vision need readers to read their books to them", he explained, "since there is so much reading to do in college." I protested that I could see the print just fine. But quickly after my first semester started, I found that I could not do the reading by myself. I could read only about four pages in an hour. So I quickly arranged to have other students read me my textbooks.

I wanted to improve my reading. My reading was so horrendously slow. I wanted to read quickly and fluently and understand my assignments. So I arranged to visit the University of Chicago Reading Clinic for a diagnostic workup. I hoped that this clinic could improve my reading. What follows is an essay I wrote about this experience.

University Book Store—a closed book to me.

The books at the University of Chicago bookstore looked like gemstones with their red, green, black, and blue covers. They lay in orderly stacks on the white metal shelves under bright fluorescent lights. Few took noticed of me that day, a pale thin young man with thick glasses and black hair. Everyone's attention was focused outside on the sunny spring day and the lines of graduates in their plumb reddish robes. Proud parents and excited college students waited for the ceremony to mark the completion of an education at one of America's most prestigious universities. In the graduation line stood a large number of young adults with robes having three-stripes-on-the-arms signifying their Ph.D.s, Doctors of Philosophy, of Science, of Knowledge.

Knowledge everywhere but out of my reach

I did not spend my time looking at the line of graduating students. Instead I moved in a trance up and down the aisles of the bookstore picking up one book and then another. My hands and my heart molded themselves around each book, feeling its size, its weight, its thickness and sensing its importance. Each book was a treasure. In an awe filled voice, I slowly sounded out the titles: College Grammar, Calculus, Human Anatomy and Physiology, The History of the Middle Ages, Anthology of English Literature, Fluid Mechanics, Business Law... on and on and on. The titles both excited and overwhelmed me, numbing my mind. *Books, knowledge, all were closed to me, placed outside of my ability to read them.*

The Reading Clinic

The time came to go back across the tree-lined campus to the University of Chicago Reading Clinic for the rest of my evaluation. I sat in front of a large machine with words projected on a screen. I read each line as the machine photographed my eye movements. I became aware of how frightfully often my eyes went backwards instead of forwards. With all my might I tried to make my wondering eyes go forward. But neither my eyes nor my brain would obey my will. A great sense of relief came over me when the test ended.

Then the examiner and I sat at a small table. In front of me, he placed tiles with symbols before me: a star, a square, a circle, a triangle. He started with only two or three in a line. Mixing them up, he asked me to place them back in the correct order. Then he lined up four... five...six...seven...eight. There were pictures to place in sequence and block designs to make sense of. This part of the test seemed fun and unrelated to my reading problems. As we finished I asked, "What's this test called." "The Illinois Psycholinguistics Test," he replied. "We can tell how you process information with this test."

Struggling to read the words

Inevitably there were paragraphs of words to read aloud. Aware that I stumbled and stopped at each word, I prayed for smoothness to come to my speech. As a young man of twenty, I was filled with anxiety. I struggled to sound out the simplest of words. The examiner recorded my voice as I read. I stumbled over words, repeated words and skipped word. Finally, tears of frustration, embarrassment and longing flowed down my cheeks. The examiner stopped the recording and put his hand on my shoulder. "That's O.K., we can stop now. I think I've got enough material to do my evaluation report." "How soon will the report be done?" I asked. "Several weeks from now. I will mail you a copy at your home." With that we parted and I took the long train ride back to Indiana to my university dorm room.

The report arrives

The clinical report was too difficult for me to understand. So, I asked my mother to read the report, saying, "I want to go to this clinic and get help with my reading. I can't get through college without being able to read better." She and my father spent the next day with the report. Then, they called me in to talk to me. They read sections of the report to me, especially emphasizing the part of the letter and report which stated that the clinic could not help me. I had something called dyslexia. The report concluded, "Since you seem to learn and pass your classes using readers, we strongly support your continued use of readers in pursuing your education."

Devastated I took the report and went to my room. Sitting on my bed with tears welling up in my eyes, I struggled for hours through every line of the report, hoping to find the answer for a cure to my reading problems. Couldn't anybody fix me? Couldn't someone, somewhere teach me to read better—to read faster? These questions with no answers swirled in my head. I felt dizzy and heartsick.

I just wanted to be like the other students, to read as they did. If I could read well, surely I could pass my classes. Reading faster was the key to becoming a computer programmer or a biology teacher. Reading held out so many possibilities. But all of these possibilities seemed out of my reach. I could not read the required books. For me the most memorable paragraph of the report was on my "Reading Achievement." *After two years at the university, my reading test indicated that I only read at the third grade level.* The third grade level and the words "we can do nothing for you" created a deep pain that shocked me from head to toe.

Reading with both EYES and EARS!

I returned to the university in the fall armed with a new tape recorder. I recorded my readers as they read to me. As my readers read aloud, I would follow along. I would also follow along when rereading every chapter of my assignments. My readers read to me. They read my books, my class notes, my under-linings, and supplementary materials. My grades moved from D's to C's to B's. I could take only half the credit load others took.

I transferred to the University of Denver. At the University of Denver, I developed my formula for getting A's. All chapters, papers, and books had to be read at least three times. On the first reading, I would follow along as my readers recorded my textbooks. The first reading gave me an introduction to the material. Upon a second reading of the assignment, I would make a check next to important points. On the third time through, the rereading cemented the information in my mind. Three readings really allowed me to digest what the author was writing about. Answers and essays now flowed easily from my pen.

Learning to cope with dyslexia

If you or your dyslexic child are told to "simply try harder" or to "study harder," this will not solve the problem with reading. Overcoming the barriers and coping are very challenging. It is correct to tell someone with dyslexia that learning can be hard work. Real learning is not easy. Additionally, a young child or adult with dyslexia will need others to give them help in learning. You should not be afraid to ask for help.

When I entered college reading at the third grade level, I wasn't simply under-prepared or lazy. I was illiterate. My journey has been a tumultuous struggle from illiteracy to literacy. I could not read the college texts. I could not write in complete sentences. 30% of the words I wrote were misspelled.

So, I had my undergraduate and graduate books read to me. This "Reading To Me" and "Following Along" experience opened up books and knowledge to me. By being read to, I completed my college degree, then a master's degree and finally a Doctor of Philosophy in Psychology. Dyslexia sets up real barriers to learning. Books can be read to you. Books can be read using audiobooks, a computer or an iPad. This assistance can open up a vast world of knowledge for you or your child.

Every child wants to learn

When you cannot read, it is heart wrenching! There are alternatives for you or your dyslexic child. I recommend reading to your child and using digital books or audiobooks. Many people will still tell you about your child, "He or she simply needs to try harder, to pay attention more, or to stop being lazy, or to do it on his own without help." Do not believe them. I repeat, *"Don't believe them!"*

I have found that every child wants to learn and wants to be successful at learning. Open wide the book covers, read aloud, listen to books, and begin the learning process. As you and your child read books aloud over and over, again and again, this will not only increase knowledge your child has, but in the long run you will also improve his or her reading. I have spent many hours listening and actively following the words as others have read to me. These hours of listening, learning, and "reading-along" now allow me to write this book. Even more wonderful, I can also read this book fluently and meaningfully to others.

Chapter 4: Dyslexia: Tips for Reading

Programs to reading

Dyslexic students generally need extra help with learning to read. Often this means having extra reading lessons and specialized reading instruction. Different specialized methods have been developed to help dyslexic students learn to read. Most of these methods use a multi-modal approach to learning. Multi-modal means using more than one sense modality at a time. For example, students look at printed letters, play with the letters in clay, draw the letters in sand, and say the letters aloud. A good discussion of methods for teaching dyslexic children reading is found in *The Everything Parent's Guide to Children With Dyslexia* by Abigail Marshall.

Dyslexic students need more intense and individualized reading instruction. Sometimes this special reading instruction is not available at public school. But often the school's reading specialist has taken extra training in these methods. To learn more about this instruction, look up the International Dyslexic Association, Orton-Gillingham Method, Lindmood-Bell Method, Barton Reading Program, and Wilson Reading System.

You may live in an area where this instruction is not available. You may simply not have the money for reading instruction. I highly recommend looking at the Barton Reading Program. You can be trained to give your child specialized reading instruction. There are ten levels of instruction in this program. Each level cost $250 and takes about four months to complete. Even though this seems expensive, it can be a lifesaver when other alternatives do not exist.

Beyond seeking out specialized instruction, the material below presents suggestions to help with reading. Let me point out that the iPad is a Godsend for children and adults with dyslexia. But the iPad is not meant to replace a comprehensive reading program and specialized reading teachers. It can, however, supplement reading instruction. The iPad's unique accessibility tools also make books and the World Wide Web accessible to those with dyslexia.

Reading To, With, and By

Several years ago, I took a series of graduate courses on the teaching of reading. These classes were taught by Dr. Barbara Swaby_of the University of Colorado at Colorado Springs. She is the director of the reading clinic at the University. She emphasized the importance of reading "To" students, reading "With" students, and then the students reading "By" themselves. Reading "To" is just what it sounds like. You read stories "To" your child. It is best to pick something really engaging. Reading "With" is reading out loud while both your child and you follow the text in the book. Reading "With" focuses on the text with the support of your auditory input. You can spend some time pointing to the words as you read. Reading "By" is just that: your child reads the story by herself. The first two steps may need to be done many, many times before your child is successful in reading "By." Dr. Swaby stated that "Reading To, With, and By" should be a practice from kindergarten through high school.

During the course of my undergraduate and graduate education, I was read "To and With" by audiobooks and fellow students for many hours. This "Reading To and Reading With" experience transformed me into a productive reader. I read very fluently at 160 words per minute. I can read in every subject area that interests me. Nowadays there are many audiobooks to listen to and e-books which can be read using iPad's VoiceOver reader. If you listen to an audiobook and follow the text for just one hour a day, you will have 365 hours of "Reading To" and "Reading With" experience in a year. Additionally, you will have fun with reading.

The Presentation of Print

Dyslexic individuals can read better when the print is arranged in specific ways on a page. Here are a few simple tricks. (1) With a word processing program, increase the spacing between words and letters. When space is increased, this is called kerning. Most software packages allow you to adjust the space between letters and words. (2) Space between words can also be increased by setting the word alignment to "full justification." e-Book apps like Kindle or iBooks apps allow you to choose full justification. This extra space assists in perception and word comprehension. (3) The font you choose to read with also makes a difference. A good font for reading is Verdana or Arial. Verdana, Palatino, or Helvetia are san serif fonts. San serif fonts have no artistic edges attached to the letters. "San" means without these edges. (4) A pastel background color for the paper or screen is also helpful in reading. Generally the paper or screen is bright white and the letters are black. But when paper and backgrounds are cream or light pastel, it is easier on the eyes and perception. Often reading apps have a nighttime setting. This setting changes the background to black and the letters to white. This can be helpful. Other apps like Bookshare's Read2Go allow for many choices of colors for background and letters.

Being "Read To" is Reading

After being evaluated at the University of Chicago Reading Clinic, I received their diagnostic report. In the report the clinical evaluator indicated that my reading could not be improved. I had dyslexia. Dyslexia is a language-based disability which interferes most noticeably with reading, writing, spelling and the acquisition of a foreign language. I also had a short-term serial memory deficit. This deficit accounted for my inability to remember phone numbers or names. This deficit is also the reason that I cannot remember letters spoken to me.

The clinic recommended that I continue to have my books read aloud to me. Fellow students often read to me. I also got audio recordings of textbooks from Learning Ally, formally Recording for the Blind and Dyslexic.

Today you can get many textbooks as digital textbooks. These can be read to you using Apple iOS devices. The iPhone, iPod Touch, or iPad have a built in reader, VoiceOver, to read books and webpages aloud. I frequently use VoiceOver or text-to-speech voices to read nonfiction books, articles and web pages. But I still prefer using audiobooks to read fiction. Audiobooks use professional narrators who add a lot of interest to works of fiction. The iTunes Store lists over 100,000 audiobooks.

Accessible Textbooks

After being diagnosed with dyslexia, I contacted an organization called Learning Ally, formerly Recording for the Blind and Dyslexic. Learning Ally has a large library of recorded textbooks both at the K-12 and college level. Some students prefer books that are read by people as oppose to computerized voices. Learning Ally uses volunteers to read and record textbooks and books. Additionally, you can send textbooks and other books to Learning Ally to be recorded.

Over the years, I sent many textbooks to Learning Ally to be recorded and sent back to me. Generally, you should send books to Learning Ally giving a good amount of lead-time for them to record the book. Books from Learning Ally now come as digital audio files. Learning Ally has a great Learning Ally App that allows you to read these audio books on the iPhone or iPad.

Bookshare is also an additional source for accessible textbooks and books. A resident of the United States with a print disability like dyslexia can get e-books from Bookshare. K-12 students with an Individual Education Plan (IEP) and a print disability qualify for free e-books from Bookshare. Older individuals and college students with a print disability can get unlimited e-books from Bookshare for a one-time $25 application fee and a $50 annual fee.

Bookshare has digitized textbooks both at the K-12 and university level. Unlike Learning Ally, the textbooks are not audiobooks; they are text files in Daisy format. These files can be read aloud using computerized text-to-speech. Bookshare scans some books into digital files and also gets many files directly from publishers. Bookshare has an iPad and iPod Touch app, Read2Go. The Read2Go app can download books onto an iPhone or iPad. The advantage of Read2Go is that text is displayed and highlighted as it is read aloud.

Machines that Read Aloud

An iPod Touch that fits in your pocket can read a library of books to you. But the story of reading machines starts in 1976. Ray Kurzweil was the first person to put a scanner, optical character recognition software (OCR), and computerized text-to-speech together into a reading machine. This machine was called the Kurzweil Reading Machine. It could process print on a page of a book and read out loud to a person. Kurzweil's first reading machine was the size of a home dishwasher and weighed 350 pounds. One placed a book on a scanning window, and the machine would read a page at a time. The original Kurzweil Reading Machine cost $50,000. The first person to own the Kurzweil Reading Machine was the Grammy songwriter and singer Stevie Wonder.

The major advantage of the Kurzweil Reading Machine was that a person could read any book at anytime. Blind or dyslexic students no longer needed to find a person to read to them. Later on Kurzweil Education Systems came out with the scanning-reading software Kurzweil 3000, which runs on a Windows or Macintosh computer. With a scanner and a PC, lots of schools scanned many books for students to read. This software costing $1,395. At this price tag Kurzweil 3000 was much more affordable for school districts. But the software is often too expensive for most families or individuals to afford.

Fortunately, now a $200 iPod Touch can be used as a reading machine. Many books are available as e-books from the Kindle Store, iBookstore, Learning Ally or Bookshare. All of the e-books available in the iBookstore can be read using Apple's iOS VoiceOver. The great advantage of reading with iDevices is portability. For example, a friend of mine who is blind was camping on a remote island in northern Michigan. He wanted a book to read for the weekend. So he took out his iPhone and found that he had good cell reception. So he downloaded a new book from Bookshare and started to read.

Build Your Own Reading Machine

Sometimes when books are not available as e-books or as audiobooks, one can scan them onto a computer to read. Here is the cheapest way I found for building a reading machine. You will need a personal computer, a flatbed scanner, optical character recognition software and text-to-speech software.

A personnel computer. A personal computer is the brains of your reading machine. Fortunately, PCs are fairly inexpensive. You can even get an inexpensive netbook for $250.

A flatbed scanner. The flatbed scanner takes an image of the page of print and puts it into the computer. I use a special scanner, OptiBook 3800 from Plustek, which costs $270. The OptiBook scanner is designed especially for scanning books. The book spine sits on the edge of the scanner; in this way books are scanned without damaging the spine of the book. You scan each page of the book into a computer folder. The scanning software automatically numbers each image, so that each page of the book will be in the proper order.

Optical character recognition, OCR, software. OCR analyzes the image of print and converts the image into digital text. OCR is basically 100% accurate nowadays. The best OCR software on the market in my opinion is ABBYY FineReader Pro. You import your scanned book into FineReader Pro, which will then turn your book into an ePub e-book. Your new ePub book can be placed into the iBooks app on your iPad or iPod Touch. Once in iBooks, your ePub book can be read to you using VoiceOver.

Text-to-speech software. If you want to read the scanned book on your computer, you will need text-to-speech software. A good product is Universal Reader Plus from Premier Literacy. Universal Reader acts like a floating tool bar. The tool bar can be visible when you are in different programs like Microsoft Word, Internet Explorer or Chrome Browser. When you hover your mouse over the text, Reader will read the text to you.

The Power of Rereading

Now with digital books on your iDevice, what is the best approach to reading and studying? One of the best ways to read is to follow the text in the book while VoiceOver or another text-to-speech voice reads the text to you. By combining seeing and hearing, comprehension is greatly improved. Additionally, by listening while following the text, you will ultimately increase your ability to read. This approach will help you recognize a large number of words when you read on your own.

Rereading is my formula for success in learning. Many students in school do not understand the value of rereading. Very good students often reread their assignments. One of my first assistive devices was a tape recorder. With this tape recorder I read recorded books from Learning Ally. The major advantage of audio and digital books is the ability to reread books and assignments. My formula for success in school includes rereading class assignments. The steps go as follows:

1. Read and study the material one time and you will get a C.

2. Read and study the material two times and you will get a B.

3. Read and study the material three times and you will get an A.

This formula changed me from a D student to a straight-A student.

Once I learned this approach of rereading, I would make no marks or notes on my first reading. In this way I could follow the authors train of thought with no interruptions. On my second reading, I would high-light the major words to be memorized. Note I still just highlighted single words. Then on my third review, I would highlight important sentences to be learned. The advantage of this approach is that it helps in fo-cusing on the most important concepts to be learned. If you highlight on the first reading, you often highlight too much material, since all the ideas are new. When you highlight too many things, it is difficult to find the important concepts.

The Power of Variable Reading

A principle taught in school is to vary the speed of reading. Your speed depends on the complexity of the material being read. One of the great features of audiobooks or digitized books is the ability to vary the pace of the reading. With a variable control, you can change the pace of the reading. On the iPad, by going into the setting you can vary the speed of Voice-Over. VoiceOver also can be adjusted with on-screen gestures. A rotor movement with two fingers turns VoiceOver gestures on and off. When reading speed is turned on, a simple flick of a finger can change reading speed. Additionally, the Read2Go app or Learning Ally apps have sliders in their setting to vary the pace of reading.

Recommended rates of reading are as follows:

1. reading for memorization, fewer than 100 words per minute (wpm);

2. reading for learning, 100–200 wpm;

3. reading for pleasure, 200–400 wpm.

The power of variable reading can be combined with the power of rereading. My first reading of a chapter is at a slow pace. This slow pace is much like listening to a lecture or hearing someone tell a story. In my second reading, I pick up the pace a bit but still pause to note the important points. For the third reading, I quicken the pace in order to review the material and rapidly cement the important points in my mind.

The Power of Reading a Good Supplementary Book

A principle I learned while in college was the value of reading additional books and articles. These supplementary books often helped to clarify key concepts. I often read the assigned book and then additionally read extra easily understood books. This strategy moved me from D's to straight A's in college.

The strategy of reading supplementary books had an extra benefit. I found that the supplementary reading allowed me to forego the chore of taking notes in class. I simply sat in class and listened to the professor lecturing—not taking any notes. This freaked out my fellow students who were busy scribbling notes. It doubly freaked them out when I got an A. The reality is a good supplementary book is often much better at presenting knowledge than the vast majority of lectures.

Teachers from antiquity to 1450 lectured to students as a means of passing on information. Before 1450, books were frightfully expensive and extremely rare. Note taking was a way for the student to create his own book to keep. But in 1450 Gutenberg invented movable type printing. With this invention Guthenburg and other printers produced enormous quantities of inexpensive books. People no longer had to simply listen to acquire knowledge. Books and the knowledge contained in them were now plentiful.

Students often lament about the difficulty of taking notes. Many techniques and technologies are looked at to help improve note taking. Often students try recording the lecture using an app like SoundNote on the iPad. With SoundNote you record the lecture and also take notes on the iPad. Later when you touch a note you wrote, the app will play back that portion of the lecture. One major problem with this approach is that teachers or professors frequently refuse to allow recording in classes.

I promote the value of reading the textbook with good supplementary materials. Some teachers emphasize reading only handouts and short sections of the textbooks. Instead teachers emphasize their lectures and note taking. This is particularly true of science classes. I find that many middle school and high school science texts are difficult to read. I often look for popular books that are well written with great explanations. These books are a great way to learn.

While my stepdaughter was in high school, I frequently read to her. We read both her textbooks and supplemental books. The supplementary books were well written and easy to understand. This increased her understanding in class and made note taking much less difficult.

Often students do not read their textbooks. Instead, they just skim their books, looking for answers to questions. Let me tell you a story about reading the textbook. My stepdaughter has learning disabilities. Her 10th grade world history teacher was the assistant football coach. He taught all six sections of world history at the high school. He organized a class for some of the football players to help them get through world history. My stepdaughter was in this class. Every day he read the world history textbook to this class while the students followed along in their books. What was the result? At the end of each term my stepdaughter easily got a "B." This is the power of reading a GOOD BOOK.

The e-book Band Wagon

Fortunately, many books are available as e-books. Four good sources for e-books are Bookshare.org, the Apple iBookstore, the Kindle Store and Google Play bookstore. There are so many e-books available one could spend a lifetime reading and never exhaust the possibilities

Bookshare.org operates a digital library for individuals and students who have print impairments, like dyslexia. To get e-books from Bookshare, someone like a school psychologist, doctor or teacher must sign a form indicating that you have a print impairment. K-12 students with a print impairment can get e-books from Bookshare for free. Other eligible users pay a one time $25 set up fee and a yearly $50 fee to access unlimited books.

The major advantage of Bookshare is the availability of textbooks and leisure books. These e-books can be read using text-to-speech. Bookshare e-books can be read on an iPod Touch or iPad using the Read2Go app. As this app reads aloud, the text is highlighted. So you can follow the text while listening. The Read2Go app can be customized for font size, font color, text highlighting color and reading speed. This level of multi-modal presentation and customization greatly increases reading comprehension. Different iDevices provide a slightly different experience. For example, an iPad allows for really large fonts. On an iPhone the reduced screen size focuses attention on the sentence being read. The iPad Mini is more like looking at and holding a book. Bookshare books can also be read on the computer. Bookshare also offers their books in MP3 format. So books may be read with an MP3 player.

The Apple iBookstore is a great source of e-books. Books can be purchased from the iBookstore to be read on an iPod Touch, iPhone or iPad. These e-books are read using the iBooks app. Apple's Voice-Over screen reader easily reads the e-books aloud and automatically scrolls and turns pages. Type of font and font size can be chosen. The background can be white or sepia with black print or reversed to black background with white print. The advantage of iBooks is the wide selection of e-books. The iBookstore now has over 1.8 million books. Additionally, there are no special qualifications like a print impairment to read books aloud. Any individual with an Apple account can purchase a book. All books in the iBookstore can be read aloud using VoiceOver. There are a number of free books. Besides the latest books, there are books in the public domain. Public domain books were published before 1923. Whole collections of public domain books are free or inexpensive. For example, the complete works of Mark Twain costs

$2.99. Recently, the Amazon Kindle app on the iPad or iPod Touch supports read aloud with VoiceOver. The Kindle Store often contains books not available in the iBookstore.

The largest repository of e-books in the world is at Google. Google has more than 3 million e-books. Many of these e-books are available for both Android and Apple devices. The *Play Books* app is available from the App Store for free. The *Play Books* app allows for font size adjustment and background for day or night reading. Books are read aloud using VoiceOver. The *Google Play Books* app is a little awkward to use since pages must be turned manually with a three-finger swipe gesture. In spite of this limitation, Google's vast library of over a million free public domain books is a real treasure. I also recommend the app *Subtext* to read Google e-books. You can import your Google books into this app. The app will highlight text as it is read aloud. Additionally, pages are turned automatically as the e-book is read. I read all my Google books in this app.

The Value of Audiobooks

With all the great technology around you might wonder why audiobooks are still a great way to read. Text-to-speech voices work very well with non-fiction material such as history, science and politics. However, text-to-speech voices may not be best for novels, short stories, poetry, and plays. For these types of materials, high quality recordings by professional narrators are often better. Good professional narrators add emotion, pacing, and drama to a book. If you want to get yourself or your children hooked on reading with audiobooks, listen to Jim Dale's reading of the Harry Potter books.

One of the best selections of audiobooks is found at the Apple iTunes Store. The iTunes Store usually has a wide selection of audiobooks ranging in price from $1.99 to $10 to $12. You can listen to samples of the audiobooks to see which narrators grab your interest. These audiobooks can even be played on an inexpensive Apple iPod Shuffle, which cost $49. High quality audiobooks are also available from Audible for download.

A notable source of free audiobooks is LibriVox, which has a library of audiobooks on the Internet. These books are classic literature for which the copyright has run out. Therefore, the books are in the public domain and can be distributed freely. This includes books by Charles Dickens, Mark Twain and Emily Bronte. You can listen to these books on your iDevice using an app called *Audiobooks*. Two really great recordings are Charles Dickens' *A Christmas Carol* and Mark Twain's *Huckleberry Finn.* The LibriVox audiobooks are read by volunteers. Most books are well read and are enjoyable.

A great audiobook reading app is *Tales2Go*. For $9.99 per month you can access over a thousand audiobooks for children and young people. *Tales2Go* has a free introductory offer which allows browsing and listening. These audiobooks are from top audiobook publishers who use exceptional narrators.

According to Wikipedia, 40% of all audiobooks listened to come from the local public library. Most public libraries have a wide selection of audiobooks on CDs. Just pick up a library card and start reading great audiobooks. Additionally, most libraries offer digital e-books and audiobooks from the OverDrive system. OverDrive lets you search for digital audiobooks, place them on hold and download them using the OverDrive app. Like regular library books, OverDrive has a lending period, generally two weeks. The OverDrive selection is not very big, but the price is right—free.

Read, Read, Read

The practice of regular reading is a great way to improve academic skills and have fun. Many people with dyslexia do not do a great deal of reading. Often the only reading experience is with textbooks. Reading textbooks is arduous and often boring. The best way to have a good reading experience is to ditch the textbooks! You can start by get some great audiobooks. There are also lots of interesting e-books available on every topic imaginable. With your iPod Touch or iPad choose something that interests you or your children. Reading will become great fun. My stepdaughter Stephanie finally got interested in reading when in the six grade she was allowed to read *Love at the Laundromat* for a book report.

Chapter 5: Tips for Writing

Let's cover some significant aspects of writing

When I went to the University, I was an extremely poor speller and writer. I remember sitting at the cashier's table filling out my first check covering my tuition. The person at the desk said I had to pay $650. I asked, "How do you spell University?" "How do you spell hundred?" "How do you spell 50?" This experience showed that as a dyslexic student, I was in serious trouble.

Conquering Spelling

With spell checker and speech recognition software, you might wonder why worry about spelling. There is a good reason. When you improve your spelling, you will make writing easier and more fluid. If you are constantly asking yourself how to spell the next word, this slows down the creative process. One of the best ways to learn spelling is to look words up in a dictionary. At first this can be difficult. You might have to try three or four alternative spelling until you find the right one. But over time you will get better at guessing the spelling of a word. These guesses add up to learning the logic of spelling.

An alternative is the *Merrian-Webster Dictionary* app. This app is free. You tap on a microphone button and say the word you are interested in. The app then looks up the word. You should take your time to look at the word. Then you should type the word into your writing. This extra step will help cement the words in your memory. This will help make you a better writer.

Three Tricks to Improve Your Writing

There are three "simple" tips for improving writing: simple sentences, simple language, simple logic.

Simple sentences are best. People with dyslexia often have difficulty writing a good sentence. Dyslexics can think about ideas but have difficulty getting the ideas written down. Frequently, thoughts are not written down as complete sentences. On the other hand, one very long run-on sentence can end up being an entire paragraph. Writing can be improved by understanding sentences. Sentences are made up of a subject and a predicate. Here are two sentences.

1. John spoke lovingly to his mother.

The subject is "John." The predicate is "spoke lovingly to his mother."

2. Abraham Lincoln was president during the American Civil War.

The subject is "Abraham Lincoln." The predicate is "was president during the American Civil War."

Simple sentences are clear. Simple sentences get ideas across. Sentences with combined ideas are confusing. So simple is best.

Simple language is best. People generally learn to write in school. Writing often imitates the things that are read. Dyslexics often do not read a lot. Dyslexics most often read textbooks. Surprisingly, textbooks are often not good examples of writing. Textbooks are ponderous to read. Textbooks are filled with specialized language and jargon. Good writing sounds like a conversation. Good writing sounds like talking to a friend.

Simple logic is best. Conversations are best when ideas flow from one idea to the next. Writing is the same way. Here is a method for making writing flow logically. You start by writing a list of your ideas. Each idea is expressed by just one word or maybe three words. You then rearrange your word list so ideas flow from one to another.

Writing usually has a beginning, a middle and an end section. So, you should arrange your list into a beginning, a middle and an end. At first writing has gaps in the logical steps. As you look over your list, add additional logical steps. You then can arrange your ideas into similar groups to make paragraphs. Last you write a simple sentence for each of your ideas. Before you know it, you have written your paper, story or poem.

Word Processing and Media Processing

Word processing is writing on a computer. The program saves your writing in a digital file. Before word processing programs, people used to write out their thoughts on paper in longhand or on a typewriter. If changes were to be made to the document, the entire document would often have to be rewritten over again. Word processing is written in electronic format instead of on paper. This is a big advantage. Any changes to the document can be made without rewriting the entire document.

One of the major editing practices when writing is to move sentences from one place to another. This practice is called cut, copy, and paste. Word processing programs also offer the ability to format the style of the text in special ways. Text size or text color can be changed. When emphasis is needed, text can be made **bold** or *italicized*. Originally, most word processors were made for desktop publishing. Desktop publishing emphasized adding special fonts and then printing documents onto paper for distribution. So the concepts used in desktop publishing were constrained by what a printer could do.

Today, many documents are not printed on paper. Students write assignments and e-mail them to their teachers. No paper is involved. E-mail and text messages are written and sent. No paper is involved. Internet news is quickly replacing printed newspapers. No paper is involved. Self-publishing e-books are published. No paper is involved. The e-document revolution gives us the ability to create versatile documents meant for devices like the iPad. Documents include clickable webpage links, photographs, video clips, graphs and music.

A great and inexpensive word processor with all of these features is Apple's Pages for iPad, $9.99 in the AppStore. You can type using the on-screen keyboard or use a bluetooth keyboard. With the iPad 3 or 4, you can also use speech recognition to write. The usual cut, copy, and paste along with text styles are all present. Pages for iPad shines at integrating multimedia like pictures, graphs and video. Additionally by enabling "Speak Selection" in iPad's accessibility setting, VoiceOver can read your writing back to you. This book was written on the iPad.

Talking Your Way to Writing

Speech recognition as a writing method is very helpful. iPad 3 and 4 and Apple's Mountain Lion for the Macintosh have dictation built into them. Speech recognition can turn your talking into typed text. When writing with pen and paper or keyboard is difficult, speaking often comes more naturally. Speech recognition sidesteps constantly thinking about how to spell words. Additionally, speaking vocabulary is generally larger than spelling vocabulary. So more words are available for writing.

At first, dictating is awkward. Writing is often more than simply talking to the iPad. Writing frequently involves some extra composing of your thoughts. Practice leads to greater proficiency. At first, just think of a sentence to write and then say the sentence. The sentences will pile up into paragraphs and into a document or report.

Nuance's Dragon NaturallySpeaking for Windows or Dragon Dictate for Mac have many built-in commands. For example, punctuation for a sentence must be spoken such as saying "comma", "period" or "question mark." Words in a sentence can be capitalized by saying "Cap" before the word. All these commands combined with writing can be a bit confusing. By focusing on one sentence at a time, you can reduce some of this confusion. If a sentence contains several commands, think about the commands before dictating. With complex sentences I rehearse them in my mind before I dictate them. Dictation is a unique way of writing. Dictation and commands become easier to do with practice.

Speech recognition programs also let you control your computer by voice. For example, you can say "save document" to save your documents. There are literally hundreds of commands. It is difficult to learn so many commands. You can start by learning the most frequent commands like Save, Bold, Underline, Italicize, Cap That and Read That.

Microsoft Corporation has spent a good deal of time perfecting their own Windows Speech Recognition (WSR). If you have Windows Vista, Windows 7 and 8 (but not Windows RT), WSR is built into the operating system. Speech recognition can be turned on by opening the Control Panel and going to Ease of Access. WSR in Windows 7 and 8 is like Dragon NaturallySpeaking. With an add-on program called the WRSTool Kit ($15), you can have hands-free operation of your Windows PC.

The iPad 3 and 4, iPhone 4S and 5, and iPod Touch 5 and iPad Mini come with Siri and dictation built-in. These iDevices must connect to the Internet for dictation to work. Speech is actually changed into text on the Apple servers, not on your iDevice. The Internet works at light speed. So speech recognition is extremely fast. Apple's dictation is very accurate even in noisy environments like classrooms. So, you have a number of good alternatives for dictating and writing.

Word Prediction

Many people are helped with writing by using word prediction. Word prediction is part of a number of word processing programs. As you type a word, words appear in a window next to the text being entered. This list of predicted words gives possible matches for the word being typed. For example, when "ho" is typed the program suggests "horse, house, how". The correct word from the list can be selected saving some steps in typing. Alternatively, when the list has the correct word, the list can simply act as a good spelling guide.

AppWriter US for the iPad is a very good word prediction word-processing program. As words are typed, a prediction window shows possible matches. After a word is selected the prediction window will then predict the next possible word in the sentence. After a sentence has been written AppWriter can read back what was written. AppWriter is very good at its predictions.

AppWriter also has a special dyslexia font. This font is specially designed to help dyslexic individuals to discriminate letters. Letters are heavier at the base of the letter. The style of the letters is designed to eliminate confusion among similar letters. Font size can be adjusted. Additionally, font color and background color can be selected. Often dyslexic individuals do better when font color and background are different from the standard black letters on a white background. You should try different font colors and background colors to see what suits you best.

AppWriter also has a built-in scanning and OCR capability. A picture can be taken of a document. Then built-in OCR software can turn the photograph into a written document. So documents like handouts or worksheet can be scanned and saved into AppWriter. The documents can then be edited or sentences can be added. Your work can be saved in AppWriter or transferred to Google Docs.

Handwriting with WritePad

If writing with pen and paper are your thing, then try WritePad for the iPad. WritePad is a hand writing recognition app. Instead of paper and pen, you write on the iPad screen with your finger or a stylus. WritePad recognizes your handwriting and transforms it into typed text. WritePad is extremely accurate at identify-

identifying handwriting. Handwriting with a stylus is generally more accurate than writing with a finger. The iPad's large screen offers a huge writing area. After writing a few words the program will translate it into text.

Alternatively, the program also offers a special writing window which covers the lower third of the iPad screen. This writing window is very handy. As you write in the window, WritePad quickly coverts your writing into text for preview. If the preview is correct, a quick tap on an enter key adds the text to your document.

WritePad also comes with an on screen keyboard. When the keyboard is active, it comes with word completion. Custom document windows can be created for different paper colors, fonts, font size, and font colors. This section was written using WritePad.

Notability

Notability is a note taking app. Notability can make a recording of a lecture or a meeting. Handwritten notes are added by writing on the iPad screen. Writing is easier with a stylus. There is also a window at the bottom of the screen in which to write in large cursive. As you write, your writing is converted into smaller readable notes. A keyboard option allows for writing notes. For 99¢ in the App Store, Notability is worth getting.

Chapter 6: iPad Accessibility Features

The Post-PC Era: The iPad

Assistive Technology Goes Mainstream

Devices and software for accessibility are often limited in functionality and are very expensive. Additionally, these devices are generally not very portable. So when away from the device, there is no accessibility! For example, a computer with accessible software in the back of a classroom of is not very accessible. The iPad overcomes many of these limitations. The iPad is very affordable and easily portable. Besides great portability, the iPad has a number of built-in accessibility features.

Accessibility Features

Finding iPad Accessibility Features

Apple's iOS has a number of accessibility options. You find these accessibility options using the Settings app. Here is a link showing how to find the Accessibility options. You open Setting. On the left column tap on General. Scroll down the right column; then you tap on Accessibility. You will find following accessibility features:

VoiceOver

Zoom

Large text

Inverse Colors

Speak Selection

Speak Auto-text

Mono Audio

Guided Access

Assistive Touch

Home-click Speed

Triple-click Home

Triple-click Home

Triple-click Home is the quickest way to turn iOS accessibility features on and off. YouTube has a great review of Triple-click Home. When you set up Triple-click Home, a triple click of the home button will ask you if you want to turn accessibility features on or off.

VoiceOver

VoiceOver is the built-in screen reader in iOS. Voice-over can read text to you and can be turned on and off in Settings. The best way to turn VoiceOver on and off is by using Triple Click Home. When Voice-Over is turned on, the iPad is controlled by special gestures. To understand VoiceOver gestures and rotor actions, view some demonstration videos on You-Tube._When VoiceOver is open in setting, you can set reading speed and rotor options. Helpful rotor options are speech rate, volume, and zoom. When VoiceOver is on, the rotor gesture is like turning a knob. You put two fingers on the screen and then turn them as if you were holding a knob. The gesture will rotate through the rotor options.

Zoom

Zoom is a screen magnification feature for iOS. Sometime different webpages or apps will not respond to the pinch and zoom gesture. When Zoom is turned on a three-finger double tap on the screen will zoom in and out on the screen. You can adjust the level of zoom. After the three-finger double tap, pause on the screen; you can then slide up or down to adjust the level of Zoom. To move around the screen you must shift the image with a three-finger slide. YouTube has a good video tutorial of Zoom.

Large Text

The iPad comes with a number of built-in apps. You can adjust the font size for these apps. In Accessibility under Large Text, you can set the font from 20-point to 56-point text for Alerts, Calendar, Contacts, Mail, Messages, and Notes. This font adjustment makes reading e-mail much easier.

Inverse Colors

When you select Inverse Colors, it changes the color scheme on your iDevice. White background is changed to black and the black fonts are changed to white. Other colors are also changed. Photos will look strange, but this feature is very helpful while reading and writing.

Speak Selection

Speak Selection is very handy. Instead of toggling VoiceOver on and off, you can select a sentence or paragraph and have the iPad read aloud to you. You select a word by simply double tapping on it. The word will then be highlighted. Touch one of the anchor points and drag to select the text you wish to read. After your selection, a menu will pop up with "Speak" as an option. When you touch Speak, the text is read aloud. You can also triple tap on a word to select a paragraph to be read.

Speak Auto-Text

Auto-text is a text completion feature of the iOS keyboard. When the system detects the possibility of a misspelled word, the system will suggest an alternate word/spelling. When Speak Auto-text is turned on, the alternative word/spelling will be read aloud.

Mono Audio

Mono Audio will change the speaker sound from stereo to monaural. You can also have the sound presented to the left or right ears or balanced between the ears.

Guided Access

Guided Access is helpful if you wish to lock the iPad into a single application. This is often helpful for parents or teachers who wish to have a child work on only one application, like alternative and augmented communication (AAC). When this option is selected, the child or individual cannot change applications or iPad setting.

Assistive Touch

Assistive Touch saves a lot of wear and tear on the home button. When Assistive Touch is turned on, a small circle appears on the iPad screen. This small circle is like having a home button on the screen. You bring up different button options by tapping on the circle. After tapping the circle, a menu will pop up with Home as an option. A triple tap the Home option will mimic the triple click of the physical home button.

Home-click Speed

Home-click Speed is just as it sounds. You can adjust how quickly you need to push the home button for a double or a triple click. This will also adjust how quickly Assistive Touch responds. It is helpful to set the speed on slow to make clicking easier.

Chapter 7: My Favorite iPad Apps

My iPad is so helpful to me in so many ways. iPad wakes me up with music in the morning. I then spend most of the day and evening using iPad for reading, writing, e-mail and even voice and text communication. As I go to sleep, iPad plays music, easing me into the night. Here is a summary of a number of iPad apps which I find most helpful.

iBooks App and the iBookstore—

Before iBooks and the iBookstore, dyslexic individuals did not have much opportunity for reading. When I wanted to read a book, I had to scan it onto my computer and transform it into a text file. Then with text-to-speech voices, the computer would read the book to me. Now with the iBookstore, there are 1.8 million accessible books to read using Apple iDevices.

iBooks can be downloaded for free from the App Store. After opening the iBooks app, there is a "Store" button in the upper left corner. This leads to the iBookstore, with e-books of almost every interest. An Apple account is required to purchase and download books. Besides best sellers, there are a number of free or inexpensive books. A search window lets you look up a specific book or set of books. There are also over 20 categories of book topics to browse.

When books are downloaded, they are placed on the iBooks bookshelf. The wonderful thing about these e-books is that they can be read aloud using Voice-Over. Once VoiceOver is turned on, touching a line or paragraph will read it out loud. A swipe with one finger to the right advances the reading from paragraph to paragraph. A two-finger swipe downward sets VoiceOver into continuous reading mode. When in continuous reading mode, VoiceOver will continue to read and automatically turn pages as it advances. There is also a scrolling mode in iBooks. In scrolling mode, no page turnes are necessary.

Books can be set to three color themes. There is the traditional white background and black font color. The Sepia theme has an off white yellowish background color with black font color. Lastly, there is a night theme. Night theme uses a black background with white font color. I prefer the third option for reading. Night theme is easy on my eyes and makes the words stand out.

Kindle App—

The Amazon Kindle app is now compatible with VoiceOver. This means that the over 1 million Kindle books can be read aloud on your iPad or iPod Touch. There are times when some ebooks are only available at the Kindle Store. So, this is a great addition for the iPad. Books must be purchased at the Amazon website. Then you download them after you open the Kindle app.

Bookshare and Read2Go—

Bookshare is a digital library for print impaired individuals, e.g., those with dyslexia. On the Bookshare website you can find the forms to fill out to be approved for their service. Bookshare now has over 190,000 books in their collection. There is a wide selection of fiction and nonfiction books for every age level. *Read2Go* is Bookshare's iOS app. As Read2Go reads aloud, it highlights the sentence and word being read. Read2Go options allow for a good deal of customization. Read2Go can be set to a variety of background colors, font colors, and highlight colors. There are two voices for reading out loud, a female voice, Heather, and a male voice, Ryan. Voice speed is easily adjusted to suit your preferences. Bookshare is free for K-12 students within the United States who have a print impairment. For adults who qualify, there is a one-time $25 setup fee. Then an annual $50 fee gives you access to all the books in the collection. Bookshare is starting an international division for those outside of the United States.

Safari—

Apple iDevices come preloaded with the Safari web browser. With Safari you can easily surf the Internet and have webpages read to you using VoiceOver. Beyond bookmarking, Safari comes with two great additional features. First, when you open a page in Safari, often at the top in the URL window is a "Reader" button. When this Reader button is pressed, the main article on the webpage is placed in an easy-to-read format which removes extraneous elements. Once the article is extracted, font size can be adjusted for easy reading. Second, webpages can be saved to the "Reading List." Once a webpage is added to the Reading List, webpages can be read even when the iPad is offline. To add a webpage to the Reading List, tap on the arrow at the top of Safari and select "Add to Reading List."

Pocket—

Pocket (formerly Read It Later) is an Internet service that bookmarks and saves webpages for you. By placing the Pocket bookmark in your browser, you can save articles to your Pocket account. When the *Pocket* app is opened, these articles are downloaded into the app. Pocket presents the article associated with a webpage in an uncluttered view. Pocket is a great research tool. Articles can be saved in the Pocket app. So you end up with a library of articles on your research topic. Pocket is also customizable. You can adjust font size, san serif font, full justification and night mode for easy reading.

Voice Dream Reader—

Voice Dream Reader can read aloud a variety of documents for you. While it reads to you, the line and word being read are highlighted. Voice Dream Reader links to Bookshare, Dropbox, Pocket, and Instapaper. The app can open Word documents, PDFs,

DRM- free ePub books, and webpages. Best of all, Voice Dream Reader is highly customizable. Font size, font and background color, and highlight color can be adjusted to a wide variety of colors. There is a special curtain mode that further focuses on the text being read aloud. When you come back to an article or book, the app remembers where you left off. Text can be bookmarked to help with studying. Voice Dream Reader comes with the Heather voice from Acapella. Additional voices, including foreign languages, can be purchased for $1.99. This is definitely one of my go-to apps. I now read all of my Bookshare books using Voice Dream Reader.

Flipboard—

Flipboard is a news aggregating application. News aggregators collect recent news articles from across the Internet. There are news articles on world affairs, science, technology, lifestyes and many other topics. Flipboard presents these articles in a beautiful magazine format. Articles can be shown in large font mode and read aloud using VoiceOver. Articles of interest can be saved in Pocket and then transferred to Voice Dream Reader.

Audiobooks—

An entertaining way to read is to listen to audiobooks. Professional narrators add voicing for characters, emotion and dramatic pacing while reading a story. The Audible audiobook service has over 100,000 titles. If you are a voracious reader, you can subscribe to Audible and purchase one or two books every month. The Audible app organizes your audiobooks and makes listening easy. The Audible app will also organize and play audiobooks that you purchase from iTunes.

Siri and Dictation—

Siri is Apple's intelligent talking assistant. Pressing and holding the home button activates Siri. Once it is activated, you can request information. Siri may search the web or locate a business for you. Additionally, Siri can set alarms, start music playing, or map out a trip. Siri is also bundled with dictation. After you tap on a text field, the iPad keyboard automatically pops up. If you have iPhone 4S or 5, iPad 3 or 4, iPad Mini or iPod Touch 5, a microphone key appears on the keyboard. If you tap this key, you can dictate a message instead of typing. Your dictated message will then be rendered into typed text. Any text entry field can also use dictation.

You need an Internet connection for dictation to work. The iPad sends your dictated speech to the Apple servers. Once on the servers, your speech is converted into a typed text. This text is sent back to your iPad. Since the Internet operates literally at light speed, your voice dictation is rendered into typed text very quickly. Dictation is very accurate even in noisy environments like a classroom.

Pages, Keynote and Numbers—

Pages, Keynote and Numbers are Apple's productivity suite. Each app costs only $9.99 in the App Store. With this set of apps you can give up your computer for an iPad.

Pages is Apple's word processing program. Pages is a full featured word processor and is easy to use. Besides entering text, you can insert pictures, videos, and graphs. Text styles are also easily chosen. This book was written on my iPad using Pages.

Keynote is Apple's presentation program, similar to Microsoft PowerPoint. Keynote can help you make presentations for a class, to a conference or to a business meeting. Text, graphs, and pictures are easily added to a slide. In order to keep on track during your presentation, you can add presenter notes to each slide. When the presentation is presented, the audience will see the slide while you also see the presenter notes.

Numbers is Apple's spreadsheet application. Spreadsheet applications are used to do numerical analysis. Numbers are arranged in columns and rows. It is possible to carry out mathematical calculations across the rows or down the columns. Numbers also can easily create graphs and charts. Numbers and other spreadsheet programs are not as intuitive as word processing. By watching some tutorials or reading a book, you can learn how Numbers works.

Prizmo—

Prizmo is a scanning, OCR and text-to-speech app for the iPhone. Prizmo can take a picture of a document, like a letter, syllabus, or lecture outline. The picture can be adjusted to heighten its quality. Then by using Prizmo's built-in OCR, the image is rendered as text. Prizmo's built-in text-to-speech then reads the document to you. Although designed for the iPhone, Prizmo can be used on any iDevice. However, it is best to use an iDevice with at least a 5 megapixel camera.

Maps and Turn-by-Turn Navigation—

iOS devices come with Apple's Maps app. If the iPad is connected to Wi-Fi, Maps will show your location with a small blue dot. When on the go, Maps needs an iPad that includes GPS. If Maps does not show your location, you should turn on location services in Settings under Privacy. Wi-Fi also needs to be turned on. By giving Siri a location, Maps will plan your route and give you audible turn-by-turn directions. You can ask Siri for driving or walking directions. In Settings under Maps, the volume of the turn-by-turn directions and the label size for street names can be selected. GPS navigation uses a lot of battery power. On a long trip, it is wise to invest in a car charger or an external battery pack. There are a variety of navigation apps for the iPhone and for the iPad with GPS capability. I also like the Google Maps app and the VZ

Navigator From Verizon. Your cell phone carrier usually also has good navigation apps.

iTunes Store, Music App and iTunes Match—

I love music. In the past, I had a very difficult time finding the CDs in my music collection. But with the Music App, finding and playing music is a breeze. The iPad comes with the iTunes and Music apps installed. iTunes is a gateway to music, audiobooks, podcasts, and movies. Purchased music is added to the Music App. Music from a CD collection can also be transfer to your iPad or iPod Touch. Apple's iTunes free software can be downloaded to your computer. Once installed, place a music CD in your CD or DVD drive. The iTunes software will move the music into the iTunes library. When you connect your iDevice to the computer, iTunes will add the music to your Music app.

A 16 gigabyte iPad or iPhone does not have much memory. Music can take up a lot of memory. Fortunately, there is a solution to this problem. For $25 a year your music can be loaded into Apple's music cloud service called iTunes Match. iTunes Match examines the music in your computer's iTunes library. If the music is available in Apple's iTunes Store, the music is matched in the cloud. Any music not matched can be uploaded to the cloud. You can place up to 25,000 songs into iTunes Match. iTunes Match can stream this music to your iPhone or iPad over a Wi-Fi or LTE. Your iTunes Match account can be shared with up to 10 of your iDevices and computers.

Pandora Radio—

Pandora is a great free music streaming service. Pandora is like having a personalized radio station. It plays music according to your preferences. When you select to listen to a genre, artist, or song, Pandora plays a variety of songs which match your choice. As you select types of music, Pandora lists your categories of music. Pandora is supported by ads. There is an ad-free option for Pandora. Just $36 gives you ad-free listening for an entire year.

Spotify, Rhapsody and Rdio—

Spotify, Rhapsody and Rdio are music streaming services. A monthly subscription to any of these services lets you access huge libraries of music. Whether your tastes are classical, a cappella, hip hop, or funk, you can find it. Each of these services has an app for streaming music to your iDevice. The big advantage of these subscription services is the ability to bookmark and play albums straight through.

Clock—

Apple's Clock app gives you four different clock functions. First is a world clock. I live in Michigan and often want to know the time in L.A., where my niece lives. World clock quickly answers this question. Second is an alarm clock. You can set up a wake-up alarm as a one-time occurrence or for any particular day of the week. There are a variety of alert sounds from buzzers to bells. But I like to choose a song from my music library to wake me up. Third is a stopwatch. Lastly, there is a count down timer. This timer also has a variety of possible alerts. But you can also choose "Stop Playing" which puts your iPad into sleep mode. In this way your iPad can play music as you fall asleep and then enter sleep mode, waiting for your morning alarm to wake you up. Siri can control the Clock functions. Siri can check the time around the world and easily set up alarms for you.

Calendar—

While I worked in an office, I was frequently asked to keep a calendar. I was largely unsuccessful at maintaining a written or computer calendar. Calendars seem to be particularly difficult for dyslexic people to keep. Now with the Calendar app, I easily keep a daily calendar. Calendar takes only a minute to check or add events. Calendar can also link to other people's calendars. So you can keep track of events important to friends and family. Dyslexic students often find it difficult to keep track of homework assignments. After examining a variety of homework calendar apps, I think Apple's Calendar is straightforward and easier than most. These traits go a long way to successful calendar use.

Contacts—

I frequently had difficulty keeping people's phone numbers and addresses straight. iDevices come with a Contacts app which overcomes this problem. In a contact you can list a person's name, home address, work address, cell phone, home phone, e-mail address, birthday and notes. Contacts interact with other iOS apps. With Siri, simply say the person's name and an action like "Send an e-mail to Justin." With Siri actions you can send an email, place a phone call, make an appointment, or send a text message.

WhitePages App—

The traditional phone book is very impractical for me to use. People with dyslexia often have a short-term memory deficit. This deficit makes it difficult to remember phone numbers. After looking up a number, I would forget the number before dialing it. WhitePages makes looking up people or businesses easy. A search box allows for speedy look up. Once phone numbers and addresses are found, they are easily added to Contacts. If you have an iPhone, simply tap on the phone number to place a call. WhitePages eliminates the struggle with phone numbers and addresses.

Notes—

Apple iDevices come with the Notes app. When I wanted to remember things, I used to write myself notes, which often were misplaced and unorganized. With Notes I keep track of ideas, important phone numbers, reminders, and facts. When I need to take a note, instead of hunting for paper and pencil, I jot it down in Notes. Often my voice is hoarse and soft, so I use Notes to type my dinner selection when at the restaurant. With Apple's iCloud, Notes stays in sync between your iPad, iPhone, iPod Touch and Mac. So now I have all my notes available in one app at any time.

My Script Calculator—

The iPad does not come with a calculator. There are many free calculators of all kinds in the App Store. One of my favorites is MyScript Calculator. You can simply use you finger to write what you want calculated. MyScript Calculator not only recognizes your handwriting but also gives you the calculation. Best of all it is free.

AccuWeather—

I follow the weather on a variety of weather apps. AccuWeather is one of my favorites. AccuWeather can be downloaded for free from the App Store. You have access to your current weather and forecast. It is fun to follow the weather where your friends and family live. You can follow the weather in different cities like New York City, Sydney, Paris, and many other destinations.

YouTube—

From a very early age my grandson loved watching videos on YouTube. With the iPad we easily watch YouTube. Currently he likes Tom and Jerry cartoons. Besides entertainment, YouTube is a great educational tool. The proverb "a picture is worth a thousand words" applies to YouTube. Whenever I consider purchasing a product, I go to YouTube first and watch a product demonstration or review.

Pinger—

If you are not ready to give your child a cell phone, you can give them the ability to text their friends using an iPod Touch. The Pinger app lets you text for free. The iPod Touch must be connected to the Internet in order to send and receive text messages. Pinger gives you a free phone number. With this number the Pinger app can send text messages to cell phones in over 100 countries. If the other person has the Pinger app, you can call them and talk for free. I use Pinger on my iPad to communicate with family and friends all across the United States.

Skype—

Skype is also a wonderful way to keep in touch with family and friends. Skype can turn your iPod Touch or iPad into a VoIP phone. VoIP stands for Voice Over Internet Protocol. When connected to the Internet, a VoIP phone app lets you make Internet phone calls. For $3 a month Skype gives you unlimited calling to any phone in the United States and Canada. With an iPad+cellular you can even make VoIP phone calls while on the go over the iPad's 4G connection. If the other person also has Skype, you can call for free all around the world.

Camera app—

I love using the camera app on the iPad. I finally have a viewfinder large enough to really see the subject of my photos. Students often love the Camera. As students go through their day, they can make a record of what is happening. You can take pictures of a classroom whiteboard or of a laboratory set up to help with homework. A number of students who have difficulty communicating often show these photos to their parents. In this manner they let their parents know what is happening in school.

FaceTime—

Apple iDevices can do FaceTime. FaceTime is a face-to-face conversation. When two iDevices connect over the Internet, each person can see and hear each other. Even two iPod Touches with a Wi-Fi connection can do FaceTime. So for people who have difficulty texting, FaceTime can be an alternative for communicating. FaceTime is particularly helpful in staying in touch with parents who are on business trips or grandparents in another city. Some autistic students have found that FaceTime is a great way in which they can communicate. Autistic students frequently do not like looking directly into peoples' faces. But FaceTime somehow sidesteps this process, making face-to-face communication possible.

Podcast App—

When I got my iPod Touch, I started listen to podcasts. Podcasts can be a source of information and entertainment. There are podcasts on a large variety of subjects from science and technology to music or cooking. A good source of information about the iPad is covered in *iPad Today*.

Education Apps—

There are thousands of educational apps. There are apps to help with learning letters, numbers, phonetics, sight words, reading sentences, math practice and foreign languages. Many apps are free or for low cost. We have covered a number of then throughout this book. We highly recommend you to go to ReadingRockets.org_for a list of over 60 apps related to reading and writing.

In Conclusion

Dyslexia is a neurological process which affects a person's use of language. Dyslexia affects the ability to read, write, learn foreign languages, and remember phone numbers and names. Dyslexia is a lifelong condition. One will not outgrow dyslexia. But one can learn to read in spite of the hurdles. Specialized reading programs like the Orton-Gillingham or Barton Reading Methods are very successful in teaching dyslexic individuals to read.

The iPad is a great source of support for individuals with dyslexia. For example, dyslexic individuals are helped by following along in a book as the text is read aloud. The iPad and the iBookstore provide access to over 1.8 million e-books which can be read aloud. When e-books are read aloud using VoiceOver, this provides a great "Reading With" experience. Often a significant amount of "Reading With" should improve ones reading.

Dyslexia affects more than reading. Writing is often a challenge. Some tricks like writing simple sentences with straightforward language are helpful. Additionally, the third and forth generation iPads offer dictation. Siri's dictation function is an excellent speech recognition feature which helps with writing. Dictation also sidesteps the burden of spelling.

The App Store has over 1 million apps. There are many apps which are helpful to dyslexic individuals.

For example, Bookshare and Learning Ally provide apps that access digital libraries of textbooks and books. Voice Dream Reader can also read a wide variety of documents to you. This app also allows for special formatting of text, which is very helpful to dyslexic individuals. iPad apps can help you in dozens of ways from reading news, listening to music, texting friends, to turn-by-turn walking or driving directions. The iPad has opened the world of written materials to me. I hope that it will do the same for you or your child.

We hope you have found this book helpful. The tips presented here are very helpful to Jim. If you wish to share some of your own tips with us, you can send an e-mail to iPadandDyslexia@gmail.com.

* * * * * *

Acknowledgements

I wish to acknowledge a number of individuals who have made this book possible. I would like to thank Mrs. Kitty Clark my Freshman English composition instructor at Valparaiso University. She sidestepped Department rules to overlook my horrendous spelling and bad grammar. She gave me a passing grade in composition. Her kindness and gentle direction made acquiring a college degree a possibility.

Though my many years of education there were numerous fellow students who read books and articles to me. I am grateful for their dedication and narration. Dr. Lauren Harris, Professor of Psychology at Michigan State University, spent a summer tutoring me and teaching me the writing style which I still use today. Dr. Lucan Parshall at the Michigan Department of Education provided me with the latest in computers and software during my career. We shared my enthusiasm for technology.

For years Dr. Mazin Heiderson, friend and coworker, and I have shared a deep interest in education. We often talked of the need for a clipboard PC which students could use at their desks for all their work and for the entire day. Little did we know that Apple would do just that with the introduction of the iPad. Additionally, I wish to thank Dr. Elliot Wicks for reviewing and correcting this manuscript. His assistance has saved me from many writing mistakes. He also provided the cover artwork for this book. Lastly, I wish to thank my wife, Linda. She assisted with my manuscript and is a special friend and support making my life a joy.

Made in the USA
San Bernardino, CA
15 April 2014